LISA KENNIS-MILLER

47 Shades of GRAY IN YOUR BUSINESS

A BUSINESS OWNERS GUIDE TO AVOIDING FINES, LAWSUITS, & COMPLIANCE DISASTERS

Copyright © 2016, Lisa Kennis-Miller.
All rights reserved.

No part of this book may be reproduced or transmitted in any form or by any means, electronic or mechanical, including photocopying, recording, or by any information retrieval system, without permission in writing from the publisher.

Writing & Publishing Process by PlugAndPlayPublishing.com
Book Cover by Tracey Miller | TraceOfStyle.com
Edited by Lauren Cullumber

ISBN: 1539767647
EAN-13: 978-1539767640

Disclaimer & Legal Notice: While the publisher and author have used their best efforts in preparing this book, they make no representations or warranties with respect to the accuracy or completeness of the contents of this book. The advice and strategies contained herein may not be suitable for your situation. You should consult a professional where appropriate. Neither the publisher nor the author shall be liable for any loss of profit or any other commercial damages, including but not limited to special, incidental, consequential, or other damages. The purchaser or reader of this publication assumes responsibility for the use of these materials and information. Adherence to all applicable laws and regulations, both advertising and all other aspects of doing business in the United States or any other jurisdiction, is the sole responsibility of the purchaser or reader.

To Bops. My dedko, my grandfather, my hero, my delight – you are what I strive to be. Thank you for your sacrifices and overwhelming love for our country and our family.

With love,
Your "Bello Donna"
Lisa

Table Of Contents

Read This First 1

Section 1: Pre-Employment 5

Start With A New Hire Checklist To Make 7
Your Life Easier

Well Written Job Descriptions Will Save 9
Your Hide

Every Candidate Should Fill Out An 13
Employment Application

Save Your Skin With Structured Interview 15
Questions

Hit The Bulls Eye Every Time With A Rating 19
Scale

Can You Keep A Secret? 23

Checking References Is Muy Importante 25

Protecting Your Clients With Criminal 31
Background Checks

A Word Of Caution Regarding Criminal 37
Background Checks

Checking The Authenticity Of A Higher 41
Education Degree

How To Hire An Employee Without Going 43
To Jail

Section 2: Risky Business 47

The Easiest Way To Classify Employees 49

Do I Have Employees Or Independent 53
Contractors?

Text Messages Can Be Dangerous & Costly 55

"Out Of Date" Employee Handbooks Can 59
Cause Major Problems

Watch Out For HR Imposters 61

Before The Clock Starts… 63

Payroll Can Be A Finicky Witch 65

Holding Back Someone's Paycheck Can Put 67
You In Deep Do-Do

Section 3: Discipline **69**

Drugs In The Workplace 71

Firing Someone, One Step At A Time 73

Nip Behavior Problems In The Bud 77

"Family Medical Leave" Cannot Be Counted 81
Against an Employee

Yes, Bullying Can Happen At Work – And 83
You're Responsible

Section 4: Employment **85**

Make Them Feel Welcome And Watch 87
Productivity Skyrocket

Give Your New Employee The Keys To Their 91
(And Your) Success

Performance Reviews Shouldn't Be An Ambush 93

Labor Law Posters Are No Laughing Matter 97

A Newer Law to Protect Nursing Mothers 99

Reimbursing Employees…For Travel? 101

A Tricky Law That Comes With A Heavy Hand 103

On The Clock vs. Off The Clock 107

Withholding Paychecks…A Big No-No! 109

Section 5: Recordkeeping 111

Document, Document, Document 113

The 4-Drawer Method To Keeping Personnel 117
Records Safe

How Long Should You Keep Records? 119

Time Sheets Must Be What?! 121

Section 6: Termination 123

The Band-Aid Approach To Terminating 125
Employees

Proper Documentation Can Cover Your A$$ 127

When To Terminate Immediately 131

Your Quick-Response Team 135

Your Employees Shouldn't Be Confused When 137
Getting Fired

"Can I Get A Witness?" 139

He Who Does The Hiring, Does The Firing 141

Another Checklist to the Rescue 143

Keep Quiet 145

Your Next Steps 147

About The Author 149

Read This First

If you're looking for a way to protect yourself and bullet-proof your business from a long list of Human Resource issues, problems, and challenges, then you've made a wise decision in picking up this book!

This book is a collection of useful tips and practical stories that I've compiled over the past 15+ years as an HR Manager and Consultant. The practical advice in this book will give you the first steps to protecting your business and mitigating the tremendous risk you shoulder as a business owner.

Inside, you'll discover simple solutions and ways to avoid being sued by disgruntled employees or violating laws you and your managers weren't aware of. You'll also learn ways to avoid being fined for non-compliance of employment laws from the Department of Labor (DOL), the IRS, Equal Employment Opportunity Commission (EEOC), or Immigration Customs Enforcement (ICE), and so much more!

Without exaggeration, if implemented properly, the information in this book can save your business tens of thousands, hundreds of thousands, and even millions of dollars.

In addition, the information in this book will help you decrease your stress levels and sleep better at night, knowing your business is protected and you are doing everything in your power to operate within the law.

For your convenience, I have broken the book into sections according to the stages of an employee's lifecycle as it relates to your business: Pre-employment, Risky Business, Discipline, Employment, Recordkeeping, and Termination.

You'll learn:

- How to plan for and legally hire a new employee without being sued down the line

- What interview questions you can ask and which questions to avoid to keep your business safe from fines and being sued

- The importance of writing a detailed job description and checking both employee backgrounds and references

- The dangers of mis-classifying employees, letting confidential information leak, and not having an updated employee handbook

- How to handle drugs in the workplace, addressing behavior issues, retaliation, workplace bullying, and termination of employment

- How to make new employees feel welcome, get them trained properly, and review their performance

- How to avoid major fines, pitfalls, and issues with the Americans with Disabilities Act

- How proper and accurate documentation can save you a week's worth of work (or more) and thousands of dollars in attorney fees

- And so much more!

So, grab a highlighter and a notepad, and find a comfortable chair, because it's time to start getting your HR systems in order and bullet-proof your business!

Lisa Kennis-Miller, SHRM-SCP, SPHR

P.S. For your convenience, I've put together a variety of tools and resources for you, like new hire/termination checklists, phone screening questions, sample new hire documents, sample disciplinary forms, legal interview questions, pre-employment reference questions, what to keep in employee files, and more.

You can find more information about these tools and resources at www.LisaMillerHR.com/vip.

Lisa Kennis-Miller

Section 1
Pre-Employment

In this section, we will look at the processes that should be in place before you begin to hire a new employee.

The information in this section will make your job easier and provide a good foundation for a company culture that thrives on selecting qualified and competent employees.

Lisa Kennis-Miller

Start With A New Hire Checklist To Make Your Life Easier

There are so many tasks to complete in order to prepare for a new employee entering the workplace. The hiring process consists of interviews, background checks, references, degree verifications, all of the forms involved in new hire paperwork, getting them a workstation, computer, security, etc. The list goes on and on (I had a four-page checklist for new employees that began the moment an offer was made and didn't finish until the week after they were on board).

We want our new employees to feel welcome - as though we have planned for their arrival; not all disheveled when they show up and there is nowhere for them to sit! Believe me, it has happened to me before – boxes stacked head high on the desk I was supposed to sit at and no chair on my first day of work, like they forgot I was coming. There is no worse feeling in the world than feeling like an uninvited guest! Be prepared!

The checklist can be electronic, in a spreadsheet version, or any format that helps keep you organized. There were about six other people involved in my process: IT, building manager, training, accounting, recruiters and reception. When I initiated the checklist, it immediately alerted all others involved that a new person would soon be joining the company so they could get started with their responsibilities. When their portion of the checklist was complete, it notified me so I could mark it off.

Trust me, without this checklist you WILL forget something and embarrass yourself on the employee's first day!

Well Written Job Descriptions Will Save Your Hide

Having well written job descriptions for every position in your company will not only help you stay compliant with the Fair Labor Standards Act (FLSA) in determining your employee's exemption status of exempt or non-exempt, it will also aid in the hiring process.

Imagine how much easier your life could be when your structured interview questions are based on the essential duties of the job, rather than your own biases.

Remember, you and your company can get into a lot of trouble if you don't treat all of your applicants in a similar way.

A job description will help you stay on point and save you time. But a proper job description that you can count on is one that is designed by a certified HR professional that has done a thorough job analysis prior to writing the job description.

A job description will eliminate the temptation to discriminate by laying out the knowledge, skills and abilities needed to perform the job.

That's what you really want your interview to be focused on: whether or not the applicant can perform the job.

If they can perform the tasks for the job, then you want to consider them. If they cannot perform the tasks for the job, then you want to move on to the next person.

Some employers even use phone screenings to weed out applicants before they come in and waste an hour or two of their (and your) precious time.

For example, you can conduct a phone screening with five relevant questions that focus on the five major abilities or functions of that job. This should take about 30 minutes over the phone to get good quality answers from the applicant.

You cannot do this without a proper job description.

It Is Illegal To Discriminate, But...

Before hiring someone, most people have an image in their head of the type of person they want for the job.

For example, when I say Administrative Assistant, who do you picture? Do you picture a female in her early 20's or do you picture a female in her early 40's?

Either answer is discriminatory!

You see, it's discrimination when you make a hiring decision based upon a person's age, race, sex, etc. You have to hire someone based on their skills and abilities to do their job.

Now, you cannot discriminate based upon any of those protected classes, but you can discriminate based on certain job types. This is called a bona fide occupational qualification

(BFOQ), and it is the ONLY way to legally discriminate against a person, although race can never be a BFOQ.

For example, if you owned a restaurant and wanted to fill the position of server by exclusively hiring scantily clad women, well you had better have a darned good solid reason that can hold its own in court as to why a man couldn't be hired to perform that same job. Take Hooters for instance. The EEOC (Equal Employment Opportunity Commission) filed and settled a $3.75 million lawsuit with the restaurant chain in 1997 that let the restaurant continue their hiring practices and maintain that gender is a BFOQ. However, they require men to be considered for host and bartender positions.

Under Title VII, the law prohibits discrimination based on gender unless there is a BFOQ, which is difficult to prove.

Another example would be a religious school requiring that members of its faculty be members of that denomination, and may lawfully bar from employment anyone who is not a member.

In all other cases, you have to hire someone based on their skills and abilities to do the job. And you get that information from the detailed job description.

Every Candidate Should Fill Out An Employment Application

When a candidate comes in for an interview, you want them to fill out an employment application. The employment application is important because it allows you to keep track of applicants, screen them for the position, and reconnect with them if their resume gets misplaced.

It contains questions that ask for demographic information, like their name, address, phone number, etc., as well as questions that ask for previous work experience, dates of employment, and so on.

It's important that your application does not ask illegal questions like, "Are you married?" or "When did you graduate from high school?" Again, these questions do not help you determine if the candidate is qualified for the job, but by asking a question like, "When did you graduate from high school?" – which can then be used to potentially determine the candidate's age – you open your company up to a potential lawsuit for violating the Age Discrimination in Employment Act (ADEA).

Asking someone their age during the hiring process—whether it's blatantly asked or, like the above question, passively pursue — falls under the ADEA. If you then fail to hire that candidate, you can be sued for discrimination. Whether you did it or not, it is your burden to prove you didn't. And that can be extremely difficult to do if you haven't set all of the correct measures in place throughout your business to safeguard from the discovery phase of the lawsuit – where attorneys dig through EVERYTHING but your underwear drawer! To protect your business and stay safe, it's smart to have a professional look over your employment application. They can quickly determine if the right questions are on the application, as well as purge any incriminating questions.

Lastly, it's important that you have a disclaimer on your application that informs the candidate, among other things, that you are an at-will-employer, that by signing the application they are giving you permission to verify their information, and that they are giving you permission to check their background and conduct reference checks.

Saving Time Down The Road

We'll cover recordkeeping later on in this book, but for now, know that whether you hire a candidate or not, you should have an employment application on file.

That way, if you liked a few candidates for the job, and a year from now the position opens back up, you can easily go back to those employment applications and bring them back in.

Not only is keeping your employment applications considered a "good practice" – it's a great way to save time down the road. Imagine how much time you'll save and how much less stress you'll have if you can simply go to the filing cabinet and pick out candidates you'd like to interview again.

No ad writing. No ad posting. No screening calls. No wasting money. Ahhh!

Save Your Skin With Structured Interview Questions

Having structured interview questions matters! You want to make certain you are asking the same questions to every single applicant that you interview during the process.

Sometimes business owners want to have a more relaxed, laid back interview and not just get down to business. This is natural because it's easier to do and it puts the applicant at ease. In addition, it may allow you to connect more on a personal level.

However, doing so can set you up for a possible lawsuit down the road. You see, if you meander off the topic of why they're there and ask questions like, "Where do you live?" "Are you married?" "Do you have children?" – you can get yourself into hot water if you decide not to hire them.

Even if the applicant brings the topic up (about having children or any other subject unrelated and illegal to discuss in an interview) and you decide to do anything but ignore it, it can get you in trouble.

Listen, knowing what questions to ask during an interview is important, but knowing what questions NOT to ask is even more important! Asking these types of questions can be seen as "discriminatory" in the eyes of the law.

The applicant can say, "They didn't hire me because I have kids and they thought I'd miss work if my kids get sick. I know this because their demeanor changed after I answered their questions about my family and my children. It's not fair for them to judge me like that!" I know this may sound crazy, but it happens all the time with companies that are not properly prepared.

When asking an applicant questions, you must stay on point, keep questions job related, non-discriminatory, and ask the same questions to all applicants. Those questions cannot involve race, color, religion, sex (including pregnancy), gender, national origin, age, disability, or genetic information. Questions cannot allude to any of the areas protected by law or other areas, including but not limited to: family, marital status, whether they rent or own a home, if they own a vehicle (unless the job requires it – like a an owner/operator truck driver), if they belong to a social organization, their plan to have children, what their parents do for a living, how they feel about supervising the opposite sex, thoughts on office dating, how much they weigh, how many sick days they took last year, if they have a disability, how far of a commute they would have, what type of discharge they had from the military (honorable/dishonorable), or if they have ever been arrested; and for that matter asking about criminal history is becoming more and more tricky, so I would avoid it altogether!

If you have a structured list of legal questions already prepared and vetted, you don't have to worry about going down the "rabbit hole."

Allow for *some* flexibility if the candidate didn't completely answer the question posed; you will want to ask follow-up questions until you are satisfied that the applicant satisfactorily answered what was asked (they may be dodging it because they don't want you to find out something negative about them).

Are they able to perform the essential job functions? That's what you need to know. Anything else is irrelevant and illegal to ask.

For a list of "The 50 Best and Legal Interview Questions," go to www.LisaMillerHR.com/vip.

Cost Of Being Sued – Adding Insult To Injury

If you do not follow a structured set of legal interview questions and are sued for discrimination, then you could be out tens of thousands of dollars, hundreds of thousands – or worse – you could be put out of business!

You see, when you're sued for something like this, you have to take your precious time and get everything ready for the court. Hours of your time will be wasted.

In addition, attorneys will have to go through all of your files and talk to everybody that works at your office – which you'll be charged attorney fees for.

NOTE: There's also a hidden fee here...the wasted hours of your employees. Instead of working and servicing clients, they have to attend to the questions from the lawyers.

Then, there's time and money for litigation – and more fees if you're found guilty.

But that's not the worst part. You will not only owe the applicant for punitive damages, you may even have to hire that person if the court rules that they were suitable for the job!

That means, even if you have already hired someone else to fill the position, you have to bring this person into your employ and pay them for a job you didn't want them to have in the first place.

This could cost you tens of thousands of dollars, if not hundreds of thousands of dollars – and turn your life upside down!

Hit The Bulls Eye Every Time With A Rating Scale

Now that you have your job description and your structured interview questions, it's time to develop a rating scale for your questions.

One way to do this would be to create a 1-5 rating scale each question on your list that will be measured against the "ideal" answer. For instance, if you own an auto repair shop and you are hiring a mechanic, one of your questions might be, "Are you ASE certified or are you knowledgeable in how to change brake pads?"

Your ideal answer (5 on your scale) may be, "Yes, I'm already certified" or "No, but I've changed thousands of brake pads over the past 15 years."

On the other hand, if the applicant said, "Well, I'm not certified but I'm working on a certification," then you may give them a 3 on your scale. Or, if they said, "Yeah, I helped someone change brake pads once," then you may decide to give them a 1 on your scale.

The candidates with a 1 or 3 are not necessarily disqualified. They just aren't as qualified as the candidate with a 5. Your job is to get the closest ideal candidate to what you're looking for. A rating scale helps you document this and how you came to your final decision.

In addition, a rating scale can make it easier on you when you go back to look over multiple interviews. You cannot possible remember every single person that you spoke to a week or two ago – nor could you remember every single detail.

A rating scale will help you compare notes and make the best choice for your company. Just be sure to identify what the job-related ideal answer should be prior to interviewing any applicants so there is a level playing field. Don't be afraid to take appropriate (legal) notes to help you remember their answers.

Notes are key. I cannot stress this enough. Even if there is awkward silence during the interview, just politely explain that you are taking some notes; your interviewee won't mind. In fact, they will appreciate that what they are saying is so important that you are writing it down! This will help document your hiring decisions and potentially protect you from a lawsuit.

Taking Notes – Just The Facts, Ma'am

Everything you write down that is in your records is "discoverable" in a lawsuit.

This means that if you are sued and attorneys come into your company they can go through your files, computer records, processes and practices, reference checks, applications, interview questions – everything – and use anything they find against you!

That's why it's so important to just document **the facts** during the interview, and not your opinions, personal findings, or anything off limits that could be considered discriminatory (anything protected by Title VII of the Civil Rights Act, Age Discrimination in Employment Act (ADEA), Americans with Disabilities Act (ADA), etc.).

If you do not know what's off limits, you may consider having an HR consultant help you stay protected from sue-happy candidates throughout your selection process.

Lisa Kennis-Miller

Can You Keep A Secret?

Once you do an interview with an applicant, it's important that you don't ever discuss the outcome of that interview with your employees or your peers (friends, family, neighbors, golf league, drinking buddies, garden club, poker friends, etc.) – unless they're directly involved in the hiring process.

A lot of times, especially in a small business, everyone knows what's going on. They see a stranger come in and they want to know who the person is and why are they there. You don't have to be rude to them, but it is very important that you don't share any information with them about the interview. Why? Because if you innocently say, "I didn't really like them" or "They live too far away" or something else not pertaining to the job, then that can come back to bite you later.

I know you may feel that you can trust someone. However, it's a small world and people talk. What if the person you tell knows someone who knows the applicant? It could easily get back to them. Then that person could file a discriminatory practices suit against you for not hiring them. Keep the interviews and your opinions to yourself. It may not be easy…but it's important.

Your Personal Opinion Doesn't Matter

How far someone lives away from the workplace has no bearing on whether or not you hire them. If you ask an applicant when they come in, "How long did it take you to get here?" or

"How far away do you live?" – you're asking questions that are not relevant to their job. If you are trying to make small talk, the weather is always an appropriate subject.

In an interview situation, the question should be, "The work hours are 8:00am - 5:00pm, Monday through Friday. Are you able to work that schedule and be to work on time everyday?"

Maybe that person gets up at 5:00 in the morning. You can't determine if that's too far for that person to drive or commute.

I used to work at a company where we'd conduct over 100 interviews annually to hire 20 employees, year after year.

Our hiring manager would come down to my office and say something like, "They've been a great candidate but they live an hour away" or "They live through two tunnels and I know from other people that work here how hard it is for them to get here on time in the morning driving through two tunnels" or "They have to take the bus to work and I don't think they'll make it here on time if it snows."

Then, I would need to stop her and say, "Remember, Claire, that really doesn't make a difference. As long as they say they can get here by the time work starts, that's what's important and what we have to go off of."

It took a few times for Claire to understand this, but once she did she learned to keep those opinions to herself and hire based on the right criteria – the job description.

Checking References Is Muy Importante

Now that you've determined who the ideal candidate is for the position, it's time to check the references. DO NOT skip this very important step – ever! Even if you are the only person at the company and need 20 new hires three weeks ago, you will regret it later if you don't do reference checks.

You want to have at least three professional references for each applicant. Yes, sometimes your candidates will put their cousin or grandma on their reference list. But this is not who you want to speak with. What grandma is not going to give a wonderful reference?

You want past employers and/or supervisors: professionals who can give you honest feedback about your candidate's skills and abilities.

In addition, like your interview questions, you want to have structured reference questions in place before you begin the calls. You're a professional. The references are professionals. You don't want to waste their time by getting them on the phone and fumbling around.

You want to find out what they know and how they feel about the applicant's skills. Focus on their performance, what kind of job did they do, what position did they hold, what dates did they work there (to make sure they coincide with the dates that are on the application), what are their greatest strengths/biggest areas of needed improvement, would they rehire them, how do they think the applicant would be a good fit for the position they are applying to at your company, what can they tell you about their attendance and punctuality/initiative/management style/team attitude. These are all good areas to focus on.

Ask questions like, "Tell me about what type of employee they were?" Leave your questions open-ended so they are not answering with a simple 'yes' or 'no'. You want the reference to talk.

"Audrey has applied for a Customer Service position with our company. Some of her responsibilities will include x, y, z. How do you feel she would perform in that position?"

"Tell me what type of employee Audrey was?"

"How would you rate her attendance and punctuality?"

"Did she show up consistently on time for work?"

"What would her coworkers say about her?"

"Would you rehire Audrey?"

For the most part, you'll keep on script for most references, but there will be times that you'll have to dig deeper into a matter if you feel the reference isn't telling you the whole truth.

This will happen, and it does take practice to get a feel for it. I've done thousands of reference checks and when something's off little red flags pop up in the back of my mind. If you do it enough, then you will experience that, too.

Of course, once you begin to probe, the reference may or may not answer you. But it's important that you do probe further because you want to find out who you are getting and if they are right for the job and your company.

As always, you want to document exactly what the reference says, so you can go back at a later time to review. However, if any reference gives you information that is not related to the job you're thinking of hiring them for (e.g., their personal opinion about the candidate, health issues, reasons they were on a medical leave or anything covered by Title VII of the Civil Rights Act) don't write it down and relay to the reference that you only are interested in hearing information that is job related and based on fact.

Just like a juror in a courtroom who is instructed to "ignore the last comment," you can let it swirl around in your brain, but you cannot use it in your decision making process. Nor should you write it down since it can be used against your company in a lawsuit.

People Lie No Matter How Great They Seem

Years ago when I was helping my company hire an inside sales person, I ran across one of the weirdest situations I've ever seen. On the surface, our applicant was a star. He was awesome. Everybody loved him. He ended up coming in four times in total for interviews. To have his regular interview with HR, to meet with the Director of Sales and the rest of the sales team, to go to lunch with the VP of sales, and even sit for a half day with an employee to see if he actually liked the job.

We were a little behind in the process, so I was rushing to get his references checked – and thank goodness I did. For one of the references, the applicant listed a cell number and a work number to his current supervisor. When I called both numbers, I noticed that the person on the voice messages didn't sound like the same person.

When that happened, the hair on the back of my neck stood up - Red flag! Red flag!

I immediately called the applicant's HR department at their current employer and I said, "Listen, one of your employees has applied for a position with our company. I'm doing reference checks, and I just need you to answer yes or no to a couple of questions because something is not checking out. Could you do that, please?"

She said, "Okay, sure. I'll help you out."

I then asked, "Is Tyson Smith a supervisor?"

"Yes, that is one of our supervisors," she said.

"Do you happen to know his cell phone number?" I inquired.

"Yes, we have a list of cell phone numbers," she replied.

"Okay, if I tell you the cell phone number, can you tell me with a yes or a no if it's his?" I asked.

She said, "Yes I can tell you that."

I proceeded to read the number off, and she said, "No, that's not his cell phone number, but I know whose cell phone number that is. Let me call you right back."

While I was waiting for her to call back, the person from the cell number called me back. We went through the reference questions and he gave a glowing reference for the applicant.

A couple of minutes later the HR person calls me back with Tyson Smith, the supervisor, in her office. She says, "Lisa, I have Tyson Smith sitting here."

Half laughing I said, "I just talked to you on your cell phone, Tyson."

"I never talked to you before in my life." he said in a pleasant but firm voice.

With an uneasy stomach, I said, "Okay. Something is odd here. I just talked to someone about our applicant and he said he was you."

Now with their full attention, we unraveled the mystery and discovered that the applicant listed the office number of Tyson Smith and the cell number of his own father, who also worked at the company. In fact, the father and the supervisor were friends. It was the father of the applicant that had given me the glowing reference, posing as his son's supervisor. Unfortunately, due to this ruse, the father was fired from his position for impersonating a supervisor. His son, our applicant, was also fired from that company, and we did not hire him at ours – leaving him jobless. Tyson Smith, the actual supervisor, was innocent, as far as they determined, and kept his job.

This is not a common occurrence, but things like this happen more often than you'd think, so please check every reference. Remember, reference checks are meant to verify information that the applicant gave you on their application, as well as give you insight into their previous behaviors.

Protecting Your Clients With Criminal Background Checks

According to TheHRSpecialist.com, 68% of business owners perform criminal background checks on applicants prior to officially hiring them. You do not want to be in the 32% that don't check backgrounds, exposing you to negligent hiring suits in the future! I would highly recommend that you perform criminal background checks before even moving forward with reference checks for your final candidate.

Disclaimer: The law on this topic continues to change. It is the employer's responsibility to show that its policy or practice is job-related and consistent with business necessity to perform criminal background checks. The EEOC guidance repeats that, "screening for an arrest, by itself, is never job related and consistent with business necessity because an arrest doesn't always lead to a conviction." They also warn that it could lead to disparate impact or disparate treatment to individuals covered by Title VII (unintentional or intentional discrimination).

If your company sends employees into clients' homes or places of business, you may be responsible for any crime committed against your client, guest, or anyone else in their home or place of business. Should that occur, you may be looking at criminal negligence charges.

It's important to know if your candidates have a past. After all, you're taking the risk of placing them in a situation that could escalate.

Now, when it comes to the actual criminal background checks, you'll be notified whether or not your applicant has a criminal record. You'll also be notified what type of crime they committed.

This is not a black and white argument. We're getting into some gray area here, so seeking out the advice of a professional is highly recommended.

You have to make a decision based on the results of the criminal background check as to whether that person would be a risky hire for you or not. The decision should be documented prior to the commencement of the hiring process, which criminal offenses would preclude the applicant from being hired, so it can't be said later that it was based entirely on the individual.

If the crime was a misdemeanor for disorderly conduct, then you may decide not to exclude them from your hiring process.

At the very least, you would want to know the story behind the conviction. Ask them, "I see that you have a misdemeanor for disorderly conduct on your criminal record. Could you please tell me what happened?" Get their side of the story.

Now, if the crime involved theft, sexual assault, or any felony that made you leery about sending them into your client's home, then you may decide to disqualify them from your hiring process completely. It's your choice based on how much risk you're willing to take.

I cannot tell you what to do in this book since the laws regarding criminals getting jobs have undergone drastic changes in the past few years – and continue to. However, I can offer you advice as a consultant, if you run into a situation that has a little too much "gray area" for your taste, to seek the assistance of an HR or Legal Professional.

Here's what I can tell you: If you know about an employee's criminal background, send them into someone's home anyway, and a crime occurs, you could be sued by your client for negligent hiring.

Same goes for your other employees. If the new hire was convicted in the past with battery charges, and they got into a fistfight with another employee in the parking lot, your other employee could sue you for negligent hiring (knowing that the employee had violent tendencies).

That's why checking your candidates' criminal backgrounds is so important, and may require assistance from a professional. Ignorance is not an acceptable argument. The courts expect employers to perform due diligence and make a reasonable and informed decision based on the information they have, and how that information relates to the job the employee will be performing. You may have two applicants with identical criminal records; you hire one because of the job they will have, but decide not to hire the other due to the responsibilities they would have.

Lisa Kennis-Miller

Too Little, Too Late Can Cost You Your Reputation, And Even Your Business!

A couple of years ago I met with a small business owner who owned a residential cleaning company. Her business was growing rapidly, and she was looking to hire people to keep up with the demand. I was introduced to her through a mutual friend as a person that could assist her with hiring, however, for whatever reason, she decided that she didn't need my help. C'est la vie, right?

Anyway, I got a call from her almost two years later and she was in tears. She said, "I need your help. I've been sued. I'm in the middle of a lawsuit right now."

I said, "Okay, could you tell me more about what's going on?"

"I had a staffing company help me hire, and they supposedly did a criminal background check on the person they helped me hire. However, I just found out that she stole jewelry from many of my clients – a lot of whom are my neighbors and friends!" she exclaimed.

She went on to tell me that after her attorney looked into things, they found out that the staffing company did perform a criminal background check, and didn't share the results, but rather told her that the applicant was "OK to hire." The staffing company told her that they didn't feel she needed to know that information because it didn't affect the applicant's ability to do the job. In reality, the applicant's background check revealed a history of assault, and with further probing, a drug history as well.

As you can imagine, it was a huge mess. Her clients were suing her. She was trying to sue the staffing company, the staffing company was pointing the finger back at her, etc.

The situation being too far along, I unfortunately had to tell her, "I'm sorry. I can't help you at this point. The damage has been done, and there is nothing I can do for you – even though I wish I could. I can help you with future matters...but there's nothing I can do here."

You see, if we had worked together when we first met, we likely would have been able to avoid the situation. I could have helped her set up the proper hiring systems, or I could have done the hiring for her, avoiding that shady employment agency altogether. (Just for the record, not all employment agencies are shady.) Hindsight is always 20/20 – and it's a shame, because making a few different decisions could have averted this disaster.

To make things worse, the client later found out that the employee she fired went back and stole from her clients again because she knew where all the hidden keys were! At that point in time, she was nearly two hundred thousand dollars in the hole and on the verge of losing the business she worked so hard to establish.

Fast-forward two years. This business owner had to take some time off, but is back in the cleaning business, however, she has no employees. She told me that this experience has affected her in more ways than just her bank account. It has taken a toll on her confidence in her ability to run her business, and emotionally when it comes to the decision to expand her business again. She has had to learn from the school of hard knocks, but now knows to look to my expertise when hiring again.

A Word Of Caution Regarding Criminal Background Checks

With the tangled web the internet weaves, if you go online to do a criminal background check you may be misled with the criminal background check types and options.

To be clear, there are four types of background checks you want to have done for each applicant:

1. Nationwide
2. State
3. Local
4. County

At first glance, Nationwide would seem to be the logical choice, right? It's not. It's the most generic of the three. You should have them ALL done, so you can get a clear picture of who you are hiring and if they have any discrepancies on their record.

May I also suggest that you get a Social Security Trace. It is very cheap, shows the past two addresses and confirms they are who they say they are. This is smart in this age of identity theft.

In addition, be careful not to become a victim yourself by paying an arm and leg for these reports. The range is quite staggering because each online business offers something different.

I had one client paying $70 per person for a criminal background check and that was just for a Nationwide check, which is ridiculously high.

You should be able to get all three criminal background checks done for that – depending on where you live and where you're checking.

For instance, if your employee-to-be lived in New York for any length of time, then you may want to get their background checked in New York and the county they lived in.

I can tell you that each state and each county charge a different amount. Not surprising, right? New York is the most expensive state for this. However, if your applicant lived there, having it done would be a good idea.

*Note: It is illegal to run a pre-employment background check on someone without first making an offer of employment (contingent upon background checks coming back clear). Of course, you MUST have the individual sign all of the consent forms ahead of time!

I have a friend who took my advice on this – and it's a good thing. She checked the background of her candidate in every state they lived in (due to the nature of the job). New York was one of them. Even though it was more expensive than the rest, she was glad she did because the New York check came back with a confounding list of charges. Twenty-two charges in all. No other check came back with the charges – but this one did – allowing my friend to see exactly who this person applying for the job was.

Of course, she spoke with the candidate about this and found out all the facts. Then, she made her decision based on that information. She didn't get emotionally involved, though I suspect she was in a state of shock when she got the report back.

Anyway, my point is clear. Check backgrounds with all four checks.

Checking The Authenticity Of A Higher Education Degree

Employers must take on the responsibility to check into the authenticity of its applicants. If the candidate has a higher education degree, whether it's from a community college, university, or trade school, you want to confirm that that degree is authentic. This is part of the background check process as well.

You wouldn't think someone would lie about a degree, would you? But it has happened and it happens more than you'd think.

In fact, it's happened on my watch before. In my previous corporate life, an applicant brought his diploma to our interview. That rarely happens, as it's normally just on their resume. Anyway, I thought it was strange, so I checked it out.

Turns out that he never attended the university; when asked (and probed a little), he broke down and admitted that he bought it online.

You just never know what someone will do. That's why checking references, backgrounds, and even degrees, is extremely important when hiring someone.

Needless to say, I didn't hire him. Not because he didn't have a degree, but because he LIED about having one.

Federal investigators believe that more than 10,000 people in the US may have purchased counterfeit academic diplomas from fake universities, such as "Saint Regis University," over a period of five years. These mills in the US sell over 200,000 fake degrees all over the world each year. In fact, after a survey from the Government Accountability Office, in just a few agencies, over 460 federal employees were found to have fraudulent degrees! (David Wolman, *"Fraud U: Toppling a Bogus-Diploma Empire" Wired Magazine* 21 Dec. 2009 Web. 3 Nov. 2014)

So, how do you verify the authenticity? You can call the college, university, or trade school's registrar's office and ask for their help in verifying a degree from their institution. WARNING: Some of these fake degree mills have gone as far as setting up accreditation steps so degrees can be verified. It is best to have a professional verify the degree if you don't know what to look for.

How To Hire An Employee Without Going To Jail

Once your candidate has filled out an application, had an interview with you, has had the offer made to them, had their references, degree (if necessary), and background checked by you; it's time to begin the hiring process if they fit into your company's plans.

One of the most important details when hiring employees is making sure you have them fill out all the necessary paperwork that is required by law. Not doing so can result in big fines…and even jail time.

Every company has different forms to hire people, but one such document that is required by law is the I-9 Form. The I-9 Form is the immigration form, and whether you have one employee or 100,000 employees, every employee is required by law to fill it out within 3 business days of their start date. In addition, it must be completed with supporting documents and in the presence of the employer (or an employer representative, like an HR consultant).

But there's a silly, yet understandable, catch to this process. When you ask your candidate to bring in supporting I-9 Form documents, you CANNOT tell them which documents they should bring in!

You cannot say, "You have to bring in your driver's license and Social Security card."

That is illegal. Yes, those are the most common supporting documents because most people have easy access to them, but you cannot tell them to bring in those specific documents.

I know it sounds ridiculous and absurd. However, by law, it's the employee's choice which documents they bring in. They may want to bring in their military ID or US passport instead. It's their choice – and that's why you cannot tell them what to bring.

Now, with that being said, you could say, for example, "We'll need you to bring in some supporting documents when you come in on Tuesday. For your convenience, you could bring a driver's license and Social Security card. However, if you would like to see which other supporting documents you can bring, please go to www.uscis.gov or look up I-9 Form. It's your choice which documents you bring in – as long as you bring an original document from List A OR one from List B AND List C." Again, this may seem absurd, but it could cost you unnecessary penalties.

Recently, there was a settlement of $40,500 from El Rancho Grocery and another of $115,000 from Potter Concrete. Both because an employer directed an employee as to which documents they should bring to fill out the I-9 Form. (*Employers Pay Big for Making Up Own I-9 Document Requirements*, The HR Specialist, Business Management Daily, 16 May 2014. Web. 10 July 2014.)

It's also important to note that someone must verify the I-9 supporting documents. It's the employer's responsibility (or whoever is representing the employer) to verify that the documents are unique and legitimate, not fraudulent or counterfeit and that they are originals – NOT copies of the original document.

For example, a copy of any document will not suffice. It must be an original. Also, Driver's Licenses, Green Cards, and Visas must be verified to be authentic and unexpired.

Any document that is not legitimate can put you at serious risk down the road. If you hire an employee who doesn't produce authentic documents (and you've verified that they were authentic) and they end up being an illegal immigrant or not eligible to work in the United States – you could be fined up to $20,000 and be put in prison!

Filling out forms correctly and verifying documentation is no time to be lax. For example, if you don't have your I-9 Forms filled out correctly…EACH violation can be up to $2,156 per form! For a complete list of Form I-9 violations and consequences, visit the U.S. Citizenship and Immigration Services website at https://www.uscis.gov/i-9-central/penalties.

And… if you have employees working for you right now that you don't have I-9 Forms for…you better hope that no government departments decide to audit you today or tomorrow because the fines can be obscene.

Remember, it's your responsibility to double check the forms that your employees fill out.

For a list of "Hiring Forms Required By Law & How to Fill Them Out Correctly," go to www.LisaMillerHR.com/vip

Section 2
Risky Business

Now that you know the proper processes to hire an employee without taking on any additional risks, it's time to look at the risks involved as you bring that new employee into your company.

In this section, we'll look at the challenges and risks of employee misclassification, outdated employee handbooks, improperly trained managers and supervisors, and more!

Pay special attention to this section, as it can save you thousands upon thousands of dollars now and in the future.

The Easiest Way To Classify Employees

Employers do not dictate which employees are classified as exempt/salaried (*does NOT get paid for overtime*) or non-exempt/hourly (*does get paid for overtime*). Many employers make this mistake, thinking that to save some payroll dollars, "I'll just assign the next person I hire to be salaried so I don't have to pay overtime." It's the employer's duty to be certain that job descriptions are updated and accurate since it's the job duties that determine if the employee is exempt or non-exempt, NOT the employer. For an example: If the employee makes less than $23,660 a year (or $455 per week), they're automatically classified as non-exempt.

Note: "New Department of Labor (DOL) rules increasing the minimum salary guidelines for salaried employees were scheduled to go into effect on December 1, 2016; however, a federal court in Texas issued an injunction putting those changes on hold until the Fifth circuit of appeals reviews the case. Employers have a few options:

1. You can move forward with your plan to change some employees' salaries or convert them to hourly non-exempt status.

2. You can hold off on increasing an exempt employee's salary but keep him or her in an exempt status. Right now, the old salary levels are still in place (see above). If the injunction is

lifted, you will have to implement changes immediately to be compliant with the law because the law will be effective at the time the injunction is overturned.

3. If you decide to change some of your formerly exempt employees to non-exempt hourly status, you can. Paying someone on an hourly basis is always okay as long as you pay the overtime.

There are different exemption categories that are used to determine if an employee is exempt or non-exempt. They are **Executive** (CEO, CFO, COO, etc.), **Professional**: *Learned* (Lawyers, Doctors, Architects) & *Creative* (Actors, Musicians, Novelists), **Computer** (Systems Analyst, Computer Programmer, Software Engineer) **Outside Sales**, and **Administrative** (HR, Accounting, Marketing, Procurement).

Administrative can be a confusing category to classify; there are some administrative job duties that fall into the non-exempt category while others fall into the exempt category. The trickiest question to answer in this category is: "Does the employees' duty include the exercise of discretion and independent judgment with respect to matters of significance?" because it is quite vague.

Now, to help you along in this process, I want to address more thoroughly one particular test question: Does the employee exercise discretion and independent judgement with respect to matters of significance? As interpreted by the Department of Labor, the question implies that the employee has authority to make an independent choice, free from immediate direction or supervision. Factors to consider include, but are not limited to: whether the employee has authority to formulate, effect, interpret, or implement management policies or operating practices; whether the employee carries out major assignments in conducting the operations of the business; whether the employee performs work that effects business operations to a substantial degree; whether the employee has authority to commit the employer in matters that have significant financial impact; and whether the employee has authority to waive or deviate from established policies and procedures without prior approval and other factors set forth in the regulation. The fact that an employee's decisions are revised or reversed after review does not mean that the employee is not exercising discretion and independent judgment. You can find my "Exempt or Non-Exempt, That Is the Question" test by going to www.LisaMillerHR.com/vip

Again, it's always smart to hire someone who knows how to write a job description – and knows how to interpret the Fair Labor Standards Act – to be on the safe side and make your life easier. Job descriptions are NOT just a list of the duties you want your employee to perform. Job descriptions include a "Job Summary" (a 30,000 foot view of what the job is), a list of the "Essential Job Functions" (a detailed picture of exactly what the employee will do), "Minimum Requirements" (an explanation of what is required – education, physical demands/requirements, certification), and "Performance Metrics" (how you measure their performance). Most employers just list the job functions. This is incomplete and can hurt your organization. You want your job descriptions to include all of the above – and be as detailed as possible.

This will save you time and money in the long run, as well as keep you safe and sane. Let me give you an example from the

"Essential Job Functions" section since it's the most familiar section. Most job functions read like this:

- Balance Bank Accounts Daily
- Create and Edit Quotes
- Process and Pay Bills

However, when written by a trained professional who has done a thorough job analysis of the position, it would read like this:

- Balance Bank Accounts daily/weekly using bank data and accounting system (Xero) for financial planning and analysis, tax preparation
- Create, edit, and approve quotes and statements of work using Quotient, Salesforce and Google Drive to create quotes and final statements of work for software equipment and professional services requested by clients
- Process and pay bills bi-monthly using Google Drive, bank bill-pay, phone and internet in Xero and appropriate vendor portals

As you can see, the functions are spelled out and help paint a clear picture as to what the job entails and includes what processes are used. This helps you sift through candidates faster since you can ask specific questions based on your job description. If they do not qualify for the job (based on the description), then you can eliminate them immediately. They may also eliminate themselves, saving you more time.

Well-crafted job descriptions are essential for your company. They will help make your life easier in the hiring process, as well as help you eliminate unnecessary risks with employees.

Do I Have Employees Or Independent Contractors?

The responsibility is on the business owner to determine if the individual providing service to their company is an independent contractor or employee. As far as the Department of Labor (DOL) is concerned, "most workers [classified as independent contractors] are employees under the FLSA's broad definitions." The DOL's successful enforcement of wage and hour law, as it relates to misclassification of employees, has affected numerous business owners negatively; the fines and back pay are extremely steep!

A July 2015 memorandum was issued as a result of "numerous complaints from workers alleging misclassification." The DOL's guidance advises the use of the "economic realities" test to determine if a worker is a contractor or employee, but to keep in mind that this test falls under the FLSA's broad definition of "employ" as "suffer or permit to work," meaning that a worker who is "economically dependent on an employer is suffered or permitted to work by the employer," and thus should be classified as an employee. (Weil, David. "Administrator's Interpretation No. 2015-1 (PDF)." *Administrator's Interpretation No. 2015-1*. N.p., 15 July 2015. Web. 04 Aug. 2015. http://www.dol.gov/whd/workers/Misclassification/AI-2015_1.htm).

Further, the memorandum signals the DOL's intention to aggressively pursue enforcement actions against companies that utilize independent contractors.

The following are economic realities factors used to determine contractor status:

- The extent to which the work is an integral part of the employer's business.

- The worker's managerial skills affect his opportunity for profit or loss in his business.

- The extent of the worker's investment compared to the employer's investment relative to the particular job performed by the worker.

- The nature and degree of the employer's control.

- The degree of special skill and initiative required to perform the work.

- The permanence of the working relationship.

If your company uses independent contractors, it is strongly advised that you review the current relationship immediately. Should it be unclear as to the worker's status, consult an attorney or file form SS-8 with the IRS and they will make a determination on it for you. If you find that the contractor should actually be classified as an employee, you can participate in the Voluntary Classification Settlement Program (VCSP).

You can find my 'Employee or Independent Contractor Check' at www.LisaMillerHR.com/vip

Text Messages Can Be Dangerous & Costly

If you are ever in a lawsuit please note that text messages sent between supervisors and/or coworkers, vendors, customers, etc., are "discoverable." This means they can be used against you in the lawsuit, just like emails and other company documents.

I caution you strongly when talking to or about others to "bite your tongue" so to speak – especially when it is derogatory, harassing or discriminatory – because technology can turn around and bite you. Like I mentioned before, document the facts and not your opinions. Documented opinions are as dangerous as an angry rattlesnake. They are always coiled…waiting to strike at you. Here are a few examples of lawsuits involving text messages:

1. A sexual harassment lawsuit was filed against the Golden State Warriors NBA basketball team in California by an employee who claims that a player sent her dozens of explicit text messages over several months. They said, among other things, "I want to be with you" and "Hey Sexy." The claim also alleged that the player sent the employee a picture of his genitals via text message. The lawsuit also includes claims of "retaliation, wrongful termination and intentional infliction of emotional distress." The matter settled for an undisclosed amount. ("Warriors' Ellis Target of Harassment Suit." *NY Daily News*. N.p., 21 Dec. 2011. Web. 06 Aug. 2015. http://www.nydailynews.com/sports/basketball/monta-ellis-golden-state-warriors-hit-sexual-harassment-lawsuit-article-1.995052).

2. Another case involving sexual harassment involved a soccer coach at Central Michigan University. It was a case of "he said, she said" amongst the coach and two of the players that brought complaints of improper behavior. Throughout, the coach maintained his innocence. The text messages between the coach and the players made a huge impact on the case, according to the players' attorney. "[The coach's] words came back to haunt him," commented the attorney, who went on to say that text messages in general "have really been a gold mine in terms of finding evidence to support and corroborate claims of sexual harassment in the workplace. . . . You look at the texts and you can see who is telling the truth." The case settled with a $450,000 payment, and the coach subsequently resigned. ("How Texting Can Get You into Trouble at Work." *HR Hero*. HR Insight, 1 Apr. 2010. Web. 10 Sept. 2015. http://www.hrhero.com/hl/articles/2010/04/01/how-texting-can-get-you-into-trouble-at-work/).

3. There is also a current case against Zillow. Rachel Kremer began her employment with Zillow, Inc. ("Zillow") on June 25, 2012 as an Inside Sales Consultant. Ms. Kremer quickly learned that Zillow had a culture similar to that of a "frat house." Ms. Kremer's male supervisors ranked her according to her breast size, sent pictures of their genitalia to her, and demanded sexual gratification and obedience by Ms. Kremer to continue her employment. Ms. Kremer's experience was not limited to one supervisor, but instead, was pervasive throughout Zillow's leadership. Privately, Zillow executives bragged that the office culture led to more sexual encounters than Match.com and referred to the internal office directory as "Zinder," named after the dating application Tinder. Eventually, Ms. Kremer was terminated. Zillow attempted to cover up their conduct by having Ms. Kremer sign a confidentiality agreement and release. Ms. Kremer brought action based on the sexual harassment. The suit reveals multiple text message and emails sent to Kremer by co-workers and managers. Many of those texts include explicit sexual advances. (Kang, Y. Peter. "*Zillow Can't Duck Harassment*

Claims Of 'Frat House' Office - Law360." Zillow Can't Duck Harassment Claims Of 'Frat House' Office - Law360. N.p., 3 Feb. 2015. Web. 04 Sept. 2015. http://www.law360.com/articles/617963/zillow-can-t-duck-harassment-claims-of-frat-house-office).

Supervisors And Managers Beware

Supervisors and managers can be held personally liable and separately charged in lawsuits in the workplace. Just because they work for the company, doesn't necessarily mean that they get to hide under the corporate umbrella if they inflict emotional distress, wrongfully or unjustly discipline an employee, or wrongfully terminate an employee.

Supervisors and managers held personally liable can be personally fined, lose their house, and much more. That's why it's important to make sure that you are getting advice and guidance from an employment attorney and/or a certified HR professional.

"Out Of Date" Employee Handbooks Can Cause Major Problems

Listen, if you do not have an employee handbook, or the handbook you do have hasn't been revised in the past two years, put down this book right this instant and contact a competent HR Professional or employment attorney and get yours written or revised immediately! Not having one is a lawsuit waiting to happen – and I'd hate to see you gamble and lose!

Here are two bits of advice I will give you right now that will save you lots of time, MANY headaches, and tons of money in the long run:

1. Do NOT use a handbook you find online.
2. Do NOT order a CD Handbook and fill in the blanks.

The reasons are endless, but the obvious ones in order to protect your business are: it has to be customized for your business, it has to have language in it to protect you across several circumstances, it has to be up to date as of the most recent laws and reviewed by an employment attorney that is familiar with your company.

There is no harm in going online and doing a little bit of research on employee handbooks to get ideas of what policies you would like to have in your handbook if you are not familiar with them.

Taking either of the two actions I recommended against is very risky, as you have no idea how old the handbook is, how the laws have changed since it was written, how you need to word sections for your industry and the liability that you are taking on if you actually trust what is on the internet. Once you have an employee handbook, it's a good idea to keep it updated. I recommend you update it twice a year, minimum – whether it's you, your HR department, or an outside HR consultant.

Doing so will keep your business protected from unnecessary lawsuits.

Think twice a year is too much? Wrong!

I recently gave a client their employee handbook and two weeks later I had to make a change to it.

Not because I didn't do my job – I did – but because of a decision by the National Labor Relations Board (NLRB). The new change had to be recorded in the new handbook. Otherwise my client would be at risk.

Laws, rules, and regulations change every day. It's just smart business to keep up with changes in your industry.

Note: If you do not know a competent HR professional or attorney, you can call my office at 724-777-2286 to set up a free consultation or referral to an attorney.

Watch Out For HR Imposters

If you bring on an HR Professional, I highly recommend you hire someone who has a SPHR (Senior Professional in Human Resources) Certification or SHRM – SCP (Society for Human Resources, Senior Certified Professional)

These specific certifications signify that they have passed rigorous exams that cover six books of knowledge in the human resource industry. It also requires them to get recertified every three years – which means they have to stay up-to-date on current laws, take special classes, and much more.

There are imposters out there! And just like hiring employees, when hiring an HR consultant, you should verify their credentials, check their references, and find out if they qualify for the job.

You do not want to bring on someone who isn't qualified. They can bring on a lawsuit faster than you could without doing anything. Hire smart. Protect yourself.

NOTE: To verify their certification, contact the Human Resource Certification Institute (HRCI) by phone: 1-866-898-4724 or email: info@hrci.org or visit them online at www.hrci.org. Or, you can contact the Society of Human Resource Management (SHRM) by phone: 1-800-283-7476 or visit them online at www.shrm.org.

Lisa Kennis-Miller

Before The Clock Starts...

It's important to develop a relationship with a reputable employment attorney before you need one. If you don't have an employment attorney, then I recommend you ask your HR consultant for a recommendation. For my clients, I recommend two or three attorneys I've worked with over the years because I know them, like their style, and trust their work. Now, you will most likely have a business attorney to help you with things like contracts and leases, but I work directly with employment attorneys. You will want to establish relationships with both. An employment attorney is the one that will be able to give you sound advice and guidance on legal matters that pertain to sticky situations with employees as it relates to terminations, leave, discipline, lawsuits, etc. Although your HR Consultant will be able to guide you through the employee lifecycle from start to finish, we never can predict when a real problem could arise that calls for attorney intervention.

If you don't have an HR consultant, then start by asking your friends if they know a good employment attorney. Getting someone you know to refer you to an employment attorney is a great way to start the relationship. In fact, most employment attorneys referred like this will have a cup of coffee with you at no cost.

This may not seem like much, but if you need them in an emergency, the time you've already spent with them can save time (and lots of money).

After all, they already know who you are and what your business is about. There's no need to backtrack or explain the basics. They can get right to work for you and help you protect your business assets.

NOTE: HR consultants are typically not attorneys, and therefore should not give you legal advice.

Payroll Can Be A Finicky Witch

Maybe you outsource your payroll; a lot of companies do. After all, it's a lot of work and can cause many sleepless nights. However, this book wouldn't be complete if I didn't warn you about some of the dangers of outsourcing your payroll...and give you some sound advice on how to protect yourself.

I want you to understand that there have been many cases in which payroll companies have withheld companies' taxes but never sent them in. Needless to say, those companies had to file for bankruptcy.

Listen, the IRS is not sympathetic. They expect you to pay them.

First, only hire bonded payroll providers, and be sure that the bond covers the owner as well as the other employees - this will ensure that if your money gets diverted from the intended recipient (i.e., paying your taxes to the IRS), the money will be covered and paid to who it is intended (i.e., funds will go directly to the IRS and not funneled into some offshore account).

Second, make sure you sign your own tax return. Do not let a proxy sign it for you. Review it. Understand it. Then sign it yourself. It's your responsibility in the end, so don't mess around with this.

I understand that you want to delegate. But do not delegate this piece. This is one of those things that you could find yourself hundreds of thousands of dollars behind in very quickly.

Third, confirm that your payroll company is remitting your taxes by signing up separately for the IRS electronic federal tax payment system. Of course, **do not reveal your password or pin number to anyone**.

Fourth, do not allow tax correspondence to be sent to the payroll provider. Make sure your address is on all tax correspondence. If it gets sent to your payroll provider, you may never know if there is a tax issue.

Fifth, request a transcript of your tax accounts from the IRS on a regular basis.

("Outsourcing Your Payroll May Not Be A Good Idea, After All." *Payroll Legal Alert*. May 2015; 2-3. Plillip A. Ash, CPA.)

In a perfect world, hiring a payroll company would allow you to delegate it all and free up your time. But the world is not perfect. People forget, lie, and cheat. Companies mess up, misplace important documents, and go bankrupt.

Hire a payroll company to take "most" of the burden off you. But don't rely on them every step of the way. Cover your butt with the steps above.

Holding Back Someone's Paycheck Can Put You In Deep Do-Do

I recommend to all new clients that they have a "Wage Deduction Authorization Form" inside their new hire packet. When signed by the new employee, the "Wage Deduction Authorization Form" gives you permission to withhold wages from that employee if they are terminated and they do not return company property (e.g., laptop, cell phone, etc.).

By law you are not allowed to withhold pay that someone has earned, unless they sign a similar form beforehand. A lot of employers don't know this law and they will say, "If you don't do this, then I'm not going to pay you," or "If you don't return this computer, I'm gonna take that out of your paycheck."

That's illegal. You can actually be fined an exorbitant amount of money. As a rule of thumb, anytime you mess with payroll or paychecks, there can be huge fines involved! It is imperative that you know what you are doing and that you are doing it legally.

Important: It's critical that you get this agreement signed upfront when hiring the employee, because they will be much more cooperative when being hired than when being fired.

You can find the "Wage Deduction Authorization Form" by going to www.LisaMillerHR.com/vip

Lisa Kennis-Miller

Section 3
Discipline

So far we've talked about hiring a new employee and how to mitigate the risks involved throughout the process. Now we want to look at how to properly discipline employees who step out of line.

Hopefully this will not occur too much in your company. But, hope is not a strategy. And hope can get you fined, sued, and put out of business.

You need to know what to watch for, listen for, and when to investigate. If you miss your window of opportunity to immediately address the problem, a lawsuit may not be far behind.

That's why this section will focus on what to do when bullying, violence, harassment, and retaliation happen in your workplace.

Drugs In The Workplace

Although marijuana has been made legal in some states, it is still illegal by federal law, and you can (and should) have a policy banning drugs and alcohol in the workplace. You should also have a policy regarding disciplinary action against employees who show up to work under the influence or who use, possess, distribute, manufacture, buy, or sell drugs in the workplace, or who misuse legally prescribed or over the counter drugs.

Just because a state makes it legal, doesn't mean your hands are tied. In fact, you should know that every employer has the right to make drugs illegal or off limits in their workplace, especially if it could create a safety issue.

The safety of your employees and your customers is your responsibility. Don't let anything get in the way of that.

Firing Someone, One Step At A Time

Make sure you have "Progressive Discipline" policies in place that outline steps to be taken to correct unacceptable behavior in the workplace. For example, let's say an employee showed up to work late. The first step would be the manager sitting down with the employee and talking to them.

They could say something like, "I have noticed you have been showing up to work late, what's the reason? Is there something that we need to help with?"

Your goal is to try to find out what their reason is. Valid reasons do not include their kids running late, heavy traffic, etc.

If they have a valid reason that you can help with, then have a conversation about that.

It is important to note here that should an employee cite medical reasons consistent with potential American with Disabilities Act protections, an employer with more than 15 employees should consider immediately contacting a certified trained HR Consultant or Attorney to begin the process of determining ADA disability, accommodation, etc.

However, if they do not have a valid reason – or if they have lame excuses – simply let them know what time they are required to be at their work station, ready to work.

Also let them know that this is a verbal warning and if this behavior continues, they are going to end up getting a written warning, which could lead up to termination.

NOTE: *Even though this first step is a "verbal" warning, you must still document it so you have proof down the line – if you need it.*

The second step – if a couple of weeks (or days) later they are still coming in late – is to pull them aside and you have a talk with them again. This time, however, you'd give them a written warning. Now they have it in writing, and you have it documented twice in their file.

Finally, if this behavior continued, you'd have to let them go using your company's termination process.

By having a "Progressive Discipline" policy in place, you've given all your employees an equal opportunity. Everyone messes up every once in a while, so this type of policy allows you to be fair (and flexible, if need be), while allowing you to see if the employee shapes up or needs to be shipped out.

As a leader, your goal is to service your customers to the best of your ability. Having the right employees in place enables you to do this.

Now, attendance and tardiness are pretty clear cut. They are either there on time…or they're not. So what about issues like performance, where the lines can get blurry?

That "Progressive Discipline" policy may have your managers putting employees on a "performance improvement plan" and giving them "X" number of days to improve their performance

(30 days is typical). In this policy, you'd also want the ill-performing employee to help create goals for him or herself, so you can measure their performance based on what they and you think they should do.

That's not to say you do not have a say here. Your job is to tweak their goals with them, so they fit into your overall scheme.

Remember, company policies are in place to protect you. Have them in your handbook, and make sure they are being enforced. Doing so will ensure your safety and protect you from lawsuits, fines, and other risks.

Lastly, it's a good idea if you also have an "Immediate Termination" clause in your handbook, stating that "It is not required that these steps be followed. Depending upon the severity or persistence of the problem(s), Company Name may skip any or all of the above steps and terminate the employee immediately." That way you have an out, and it is understood that anyone who severely "crosses the line" will have immediate action taken against them. You may also want to give a few examples of what would elicit said action, such as: falsification of timekeeping or other records, theft, insubordination, unethical behavior, etc.

This type of policy gives you an out. And, you want an out. Because if an employees does something extreme, like commit a crime at work, engage in violent behavior, etc., you want to be able to fire them on the spot without repercussions.

You can find my "Employee Counseling Form" by going to www.LisaMillerHR.com/vip

Strategic Coordination Is Key When Terminating Employees

When you are going through the termination process with an employee, it's extremely important to coordinate with your team (security, technology, managers, etc.) and lay out all the details ahead of time.

For example, at one company I worked with, we would coordinate with the immediate supervisor, HR and the CIO (Chief Information Officer). Each one of us would know what time the employee would be fired, so our process would limit distraction and collateral damage.

Their supervisor would have them report to HR. I would inform them that they were being fired. And our CIO would shut down their access to our computer systems while I was speaking to them.

That way, our other employees' work flow wouldn't be interrupted, and the fired employee could not get back into our systems and wreak havoc, steal contacts, or do any other malicious act.

Remember this: You never know what a person is capable of until you back them into a corner.

Firing someone is an unfortunate part of business. It's not fun and you're typically seen as the "bad guy" by others. In addition, you're putting the now-ex-employee in a bad position. They can strike back at you hard and fast if you're not prepared for it.

Nip Behavior Problems In The Bud

When you have a behavior problem with an employee, it's imperative that you deal with it as soon as possible. Don't let it fester. Don't let it marinate. Stop it immediately. Behavior issues can and will destroy morale in the workplace. This can have devastating results on your other employees, your bottom-line, and much more.

For example, if you do not handle a behavior problem immediately, employees who stick to the rules may become bitter. You don't want this. After all, those employees may be good workers, but their emotions are getting the best of them. They feel betrayed. Not appreciated. And, possibly, may even feel punished for doing good. Nothing kills productivity like bad morale.

So, how do you handle behavior issues? Simple. You first want to meet with the employee right when the behavior is noticed or when it is brought to your attention.

It's human nature to want to avoid confrontation. However, you are not doing anybody any favors by delaying discipline. Talk to them immediately.

Describe the unacceptable behavior. Then, allow them to speak. Ask them why it is happening. Make them feel "heard." But then firmly state that it needs to stop immediately.

Don't sandwich it. Some people think that sandwiching the blow in between two "nice" comments is good. It's not. It's easy for the disciplinarian. But doing so will not allow them to hear what they need to hear.

For example, "You are a wonderfully productive employee, but I really need you to quit punching your coworkers. By the way, great job on that report last week." What is the employee going to hear? "Great job on that report last week" or "You need to stop punching your coworkers"?

They are going to hear what they WANT to hear – not necessarily what you NEED them to hear. Don't sandwich it. Get right to the point. Be firm. Tell them the behavior needs to stop immediately.

Also, give specific examples of what they have done that is not kosher. Tell them how it is affecting the workplace and what consequences it could have. Then, get the employee to acknowledge what they have done and the best course of action, so they take ownership of it.

Finally, document the conversation and what was done, what you said, what happened, and the outcome.

You can find my "Employee Counseling Form" by going to www.LisaMillerHR.com/vip

Managers And Supervisors Must Be Trained

It's important that your managers and supervisors are thoroughly trained in all of your policies, especially when it comes to discipline and termination. This will protect you in the long haul from fines and lawsuits.

If you don't have the knowledge on legal hiring, discipline, and termination procedures, you may want to consider bringing in an expert to train your managers and supervisors in those areas. That way, they know exactly what to do when those situations arise – and they will arise.

"Family Medical Leave" Cannot Be Counted Against an Employee

An employer is not allowed to consider family medical leave as a negative factor in any employment action, such as hiring, firing, promoting, or disciplining.

Yes, it's not ideal for an employee to be away for any length of time. However, matters that fall under "family medical leave" – deaths, chronic illnesses and other serious health conditions – protect your employee.

It's important that you know this and do not use this time away against them because it is illegal to discriminate against them based solely on Family Medical Leave Act (FMLA) – and could cost you thousands of dollars if you do.

With that said, if you have reason to believe an employee is abusing their leave, you have the right to request verification from a healthcare provider or better yet, require your employees to check in with you via telephone on a daily basis while they are away on leave. The person that has the power to discipline the employee should NOT be the person who has the employee's medical information. In many cases, in smaller businesses, there are not several layers of management to handle these scenarios, so a good rule of thumb is to make your best effort to have a partner, consultant, or other manager handle medical-related information while you handle the discipline (and do NOT discuss any medical information with that person about the employee because it could be used against you later in a wrongful termination lawsuit).

NOTE: When I say "you," I'm referring to the person who is permitted to see the medical information (not the employee's supervisor or the owner of the company).

For example, if your employee is helping their mother with cancer treatments, but you find out they are doing something else – which brings doubt into your mind – you have the right to get certification from their mother's physician.

If the certification is insufficient or incomplete, you must let the employee know in writing what is missing and provide them with seven calendar days to fix the deficiency. If the certification is still not sufficient, then you may take action on this behavior.

For more information regarding this issue, please go to www.dol.gov/whd/fmla/

Yes, Bullying Can Happen At Work – And You're Responsible

No one likes to be bullied, physically, verbally, or electronically, or to feel awkward – especially at work where they're supposed to feel safe and secure. That's why it's important you are aware of any such incidences.

From one employee making fun of another employee, to offensive posters on the wall or on screen savers, to third party individuals making derogatory remarks or outright sexual harassment.

These all constitute a "hostile work environment" and open your business up to lawsuits.

If an employee brings a complaint of sexual harassment or hostile work environment to you, as an employer you are required to do a quick and thorough investigation. This means you have 24 hours to investigate the situation and take action.

You need to know what type of investigation needs to be done, who needs to be talked to, what questions need to be asked, how they can and cannot be asked – and the list goes on and on.

This topic is beyond the scope of this book. You need to know exactly what you are doing and how to protect yourself. If you do not, then hiring a specialist is advisable.

Just Because Someone Picks A Fight Doesn't Mean You Can Retaliate

When someone files a complaint, it's your job to get to the bottom of it - to find out if it's true or false - and to make sure it's resolved either way. No one likes to be a victim, and it's your job to make sure your employees don't feel victimized, in any way.

At the same time, you also have to be cautious of your actions, and especially the actions of your supervisors or managers. Meaning, if a complaint is filed and the culprit is a supervisor, the supervisor may retaliate in some way against the employee filing the complaint. This could easily set you up for a lawsuit. Maybe the supervisor is retaliating on purpose. Maybe not. Whatever their intent...YOU are responsible for them and their actions.

For example, from the time the employee (who filed a complaint) started working for you, they were allowed to take their lunch break anytime they wanted. Then, after they brought up a harassment claim to HR about their supervisor harassing them, the supervisor tells them that they're only allowed to take lunch from 12:00 PM-1:00 PM. That is a change in their work schedule. Therefore, it could be seen as retaliation and that could cost you thousands of dollars in a lawsuit. Not to mention, your company could be dragged through the mud in the media – and who knows the collateral damage that could cause.

Bottom line: treat every complaint seriously and resolve the issue immediately – without purposely or accidentally punishing the employee who filed the complaint.

Section 4
Employment

You now have the tools to hire a new employee, mitigate your risks, and properly handle disciplinary actions.

In this section, we'll look at how you can keep your top talent and stop your competition from whisking them away.

Look, in order to attract and retain top talent, you must commit to being a company worth committing to. Top talent is going to know whether or not they should stay with you and fight for your cause. They have worked in top-quality companies and recognize what culture and energy they possess.

To keep them on your team, you must have your act together and present them with the greatest opportunity for their future. And that starts with a good foundation built on solid, proven human resource principles.

Lisa Kennis-Miller

Make Them Feel Welcome And Watch Productivity Skyrocket

Have you ever dated someone and met their family? If the family members were friendly and inviting, then you probably felt comfortable and relaxed. However, if the family members were standoffish and smug, then you probably sat quietly, staying in your shell and counting the seconds until it was time to leave.

The same concept applies to a company. When a new hire comes into a company, they have one of two experiences:

#1: They are welcomed with open arms, shown around and introduced to everybody. Their desk is set up and they have a place to sit. They feel welcome and ready to work.

OR

#2: They show up and meet one person. They're ushered through the office, never meeting anyone. People are looking at them like, "what are they doing here?" There is no place for them to sit. They feel awkward and like an outsider and may not even know where the restroom is when they need it!

Put yourself in your new employee's shoes. If you're treated like an outsider, then you feel self-conscious and unwelcome. By the way, these feelings don't increase productivity. They dramatically decrease it!

On the other hand, if you were treated with warmth and respect, then you'd feel welcome, appreciated, and ready to give back (i.e., work).

That feeling is only accomplished when you have an "Onboarding Process."

Your "Onboarding Process" should also include training and culture awareness. They should learn your mission, understand your vision, and know the strategic plan moving forward. You can also get them involved in a committee if you have one.

Bottom line: Make sure you make them feel welcome and included in the company.

The Strategic Chain Reaction For Ultimate Productivity

When I work with my clients, we set up systems and processes to control the new employee experience and create productive workers from minute one. For example, one company I helped with new hires now has a system in place that triggers a chain reaction for others in the company who need to be involved...to make the new hire successful faster.

Their system starts with Human Resources and spirals out from there. For instance, from the time it is determined that a hire is necessary, IT is notified so they can order a computer and set up the right user settings; a checklist is started with HR for recruiting and paperwork and the hiring manager is notified to get training set up, as well as get a desk, a computer, a phone, etc. ready for the new employee's first day; and the billing manager is notified to get all the necessary paperwork in order. They even take the new employee around and introduce them to every single person in the company (over 200). The day the employee starts, they are taken to lunch with the entire department (paid for by the company) and get to know who they will be working with.

This is all done to make the new employee feel welcome, to get the other workers acclimated to the new employee, and to make sure everyone – new and existing employees – is as comfortable and productive as possible!

Give Your New Employee The Keys To Their (And Your) Success

It's important for you to review the new employee's job duties with them on the first day, as well as review what is expected of them and demonstrate how to correctly do the job.

You hired them to do a job. However, that doesn't mean they'll do it the exact way you want them to. Don't leave things to chance if it's important to you and the company. Walk them through it. Show them exactly what needs to be done and how you'd like them to do it.

A good way of doing this – that's both enjoyable and not condescending – is to have them "job shadow" an excellent employee for a period of time. They can build a relationship and talk through situations that arise. As a side benefit, the other employee will actually get better at their job and may be able to move into a training role in the future – if that makes sense for your company.

Everybody learns differently. Some get it after watching someone else. Some have to listen to what needs to be done so they understand. Some actually have to do it to comprehend it. Whatever the case may be – and it's different for each employee – the person training the new employee must understand this and be open and willing to change methods if their teaching style doesn't mesh with the new employee's.

The goal is to make sure the new employee knows exactly what you want them to do and how you want them to do it. By having a conversation about their learning style, you (or the trainer) can save a lot of time, energy, and frustration.

In addition, you should have processes in place (i.e. a training manual) that your new employee can follow to the letter, and that your trainer can show them as they teach them what to do. I'd even argue that your training manuals should be so well done that your new employee can sit down with the manual, open it up, and complete the job exactly how you want it done.

By giving your new employees the keys to their success, you'll save yourself a lot of time, money, and resources. After all, the time and cost of hiring someone is close to $4000.

Do you have an extra $4000 to flush down the drain? And even if you did, would you want to? I don't think so. It's easier to just get them set up and acclimated from the get-go.

Performance Reviews Shouldn't Be An Ambush

It's important to make sure you (or a manager) are giving regular feedback to your employees – both good and bad. Of course, the more good feedback you're able to give, the better your employee will perform. Positive reinforcement is a proven method to get more out of your employees.

Comments like, "You're doing a fantastic job with getting your monthly reports in on time" and "We appreciate you stepping up and working so hard while Erin has been out on leave" – should be a common occurrence. Be certain to give regular and SPECIFIC feedback. Studies show that generic comments like "Good job" or "nice work" don't mean anything to employees when it comes to motivating them because it is not specific for the behavior they are being praised for.

However, if they are not doing something correctly, you don't want to wait until the review to smash them. You want to make sure you tell them immediately.

First, correcting something immediately stops them from creating a bad habit. If you want something done a certain way you have to let them know.

Second, there is a saying that every manager should know: "No review should ever be a surprise!"

An employee should know exactly what they're walking into when they are up for a performance review with their manager. Feedback should never be a surprise. Remember, it's called a performance review, not a performance surprise. However, for employees who have been under a performance improvement plan and whose performance is not improving after receiving coaching, the feedback in the review should reflect those results and be clear enough for the employee to understand the writing on the wall.

A manager should always review and give constant feedback to their employees to help make them better. They are there to guide and mentor them to be the best they can be.

Giving Constructive Criticism Takes Practice

It's easy to give positive feedback – though it does take practice to give it on a regular basis. Constructive criticism, on the other hand, isn't so easy to give for some people.

Let's face it; it's human nature to want to avoid conflict and confrontation. And that's exactly why most managers do not enjoy giving it. Instead, they try to soften the blow. They do not address issues head on. However, when an employee does something wrong, the best thing you can do is bring it to their attention in a professional, non-confrontational manner.

For example, you can say something like, "You know, I've noticed that there is an area that you could potentially improve on and I would like to help you with that." Approach them in a way that shows you are supportive and that you are willing to help them. Not in a way that you are being critical or demeaning.

In addition, you can ask them for their feedback before you give them yours. Ask them if they feel they could improve in a specific area. Then, ask how they think they can improve in that area. They are probably aware of a skill set or area they lack in. Most people are. If they give you that honest feedback, then you usually will just need to confirm that you will support them in improving. After all, they already know where they lack, now they know that you know.

The real problem lies when they are unaware that they need help. If they are truly unaware, then you can offer your feedback in a professional manner. You can say something like, "Well, maybe I didn't train you correctly in that area," or "Perhaps I didn't show you everything I needed to show you there." Continue with, "Why don't I set some time aside to mentor you a little bit in that area."

Believe it or not, the employee will appreciate your honestly and your help – if you are considerate and not condescending.

Admittedly, that takes practice and you (or your manager) probably won't do it very well the first time. It's a skill set. You can learn how to do it properly if you feel uneasy with it – or if you want to be the best manager of people possible (which I surely recommend).

Bottom line: Give both good and bad feedback in a professional manner, so your employees know that you care and so they can do the work the way you want it done.

Labor Law Posters Are No Laughing Matter

You are required by law to have up-to-date state and federal labor law posters up in a common break room area, where your employees can see them and read them.

You can access labor law posters by going to the Department of Labor website. http://www.dol.gov/oasam/boc/osdbu/sbrefa/poster/matrix.htm

Laws do change from time to time, so please protect yourself by making sure you have up-to-date state and federal labor law posters.

I recommend you work with an HR Professional, or get your posters from a place that will notify you when those updates occur.

Lisa Kennis-Miller

A Newer Law To Protect Nursing Mothers

A fairly new law (as of the writing of this book) requires that you offer lactation breaks to new nursing mothers during the first year after birth to express breast milk.

Those breaks can be just a regular 20-minute break. However, the law states that you must designate a room (that is not a restroom) with a receptacle and separate refrigerator for them to store the milk in.

It is the employee's (the mother's) responsibility to label that milk and to dispose of it when necessary.

Note: Please make sure you include this in your current employee handbook as a policy.

Lisa Kennis-Miller

Reimbursing Employees... For Travel?

By law you must reimburse all of your employees for business related expenses – no matter how nominal those expenses are. For example, let's say you have an employee who travels to the post office every day to get the company's mail. You are required to pay their mileage from the company site to the post office and back to the company. It doesn't matter if it is a mile away. It doesn't matter if they do it every day or once a month. You are responsible, as the business owner, to reimburse them for the mileage.

Therefore, you should have a policy in your handbook that addresses reimbursement of business-related expenses.

Moreover, you can get into a lot more trouble if you do not reimburse non-exempt employees whose hourly pay dips below minimum wage because of the unpaid expense.

For instance, if you have a non-exempt employee that is making $7.25 an hour (which is minimum wage at the time of this writing) who is traveling to the post office every day, and you're not reimbursing them, their pay may dip below minimum wage.

This is a red flag and highly illegal if you are not reimbursing your employees. Protect yourself with a policy in your handbook on how they will be reimbursed and what they have to do to receive reimbursement.

Lisa Kennis-Miller

Note: Please make sure you include this in your current employee handbook as a policy.

A Tricky Law That Comes With A Heavy Hand

The Americans with Disabilities Act (ADA) is a federal law that requires employers with 15 or more employees to not discriminate against applicants or employees with a disability or a perceived disability.

Here's the kicker and why you have to be so careful: it has been found that nearly 20% of the population could fall into this category! That means one out of five of your employees or applicants could be disabled or have a perceived disability.

The National Service Inclusion Project reports that 29% of disabled adults work full or part time. ("NSIP - Basic Facts: People with Disabilities." *NSIP - Basic Facts: People with Disabilities.* Web. 29 Feb. 2016. http://www.serviceandinclusion.org/index.php?page=basic.) And...if you or your staff handles a situation the wrong way...you could be sued and see the heavy hand of the law. Let me give you some examples that could save you thousands:

Example #1: Let's say an applicant had a job interview at your company, but before they came to the interview they had a dentist appointment for a routine tooth extraction.

During the appointment, the dentist accidentally hits a nerve in their jaw and partially paralyzes their face, so the edge of their mouth droops, just a little bit.

Now, it doesn't affect their speech, but you or your hiring manager notices and you decide not to hire the applicant.

All is fine until the hiring manager opens their mouth to another employee about how something was wrong with that applicant's face. Unbeknownst to the manager, the employee is neighbors with the applicant and tells them about the conversation.

That could be seen as a violation of the ADA (perceived disability) and they could file a suit against your company under the Americans with Disabilities Act based on the second-hand knowledge they have as to why they were not hired for the position.

Example #2: Let's say you have a current employee who's coming to work late every day. Your manager brings them in and says, "Why are you coming to work late every day? You have to be here by 9:00 AM. Why are you late?"

The employee replies with, "I'm having issues with my sleep."

Instead of asking them if there is a medical reason why they're coming to work late (or a medical condition they need to be aware of), the manager retorts with "I don't care what you do, you better wake up and get here on time."

Later, the employee sues you because they have narcolepsy and are covered under the ADA.

Do these examples seem far-fetched? They're both true stories. In fact, the second example almost happened to one of my clients.

Had I had not been brought in, the employer could easily have faced a lawsuit costing them hundreds of thousands of dollars. But instead of getting sued, I got all the necessary paperwork in order and the situation under control.

The bottom line: If you are in doubt about what could fall under the ADA and could get you sued, please contact a trusted source and find out the facts before it's too late. ("Americans with Disabilities Act of 1990, AS AMENDED with ADA Amendments Act of 2008." Web. 29 Feb. 2016. http://www.ada.gov/pubs/adastatute08.htm#12112.)

Making Reasonable Accommodations

The ADA states that you cannot legally discriminate against someone that has a disability or perceived disability as long as they are able to perform the essential functions of the job – with or without reasonable accommodation.

An example of a reasonable accommodation would be: an employee of yours, unfortunately, just suffered a stroke and they aren't able to lift their arm up to their desk to type (which is part of their essential job function). So, to accommodate them, you replace their desk keyboard with a wireless keyboard that allows them to type on their lap. That accommodation is possible and reasonable.

On the other hand, let's say your building doesn't have an elevator (and it's not required to) and you have an employee who injures himself to the point that they have to use a wheel chair. Installing an elevator just for them can be considered an unreasonable accommodation, as it puts an undue financial demand on the employer.

> However, you still have to be careful because there are ways around installing an elevator, like allowing the employee to telecommute or work on the first floor, which would turn this situation into a reasonable accommodation.
>
> Again, like any issue that could concern the ADA, please consult with an attorney or experienced HR professional before you make the decision of whether an accommodation is reasonable or not. If you're wrong, then it could cost you thousands of dollars (or more) in penalties.

On The Clock vs. Off The Clock

Sometimes when I go into a new client's office and ask, "How do you keep your time records?" they reply with, "Oh, my employees just tell me how long they've worked this week and I record it in our system."

If you're unaware, wages and payroll are scrutinized under a microscope and carry hefty fines if improperly reported. You are required by law to keep time records – which means that you either need a time clock, a computer system where they electronically sign in, or a sheet of paper where they manually sign in.

Whatever you decide to use, you must track the employee's name, their times in and times out, the date, what week it is, and the total hours for that day, and it must be verified by the employee and a supervisor for each pay period.

Keeping records like this is especially important if you have non-exempt employees because these types of employees are paid overtime for hours worked above the mark set by the state. Some states gauge overtime by hours per day; some states, like Pennsylvania, go by hours per week.

In addition, there are numerous other reasons to know when an employee is on the clock and when they are off the clock.

For example, let's say you own a mining company, where your employees have to put on protective gear to work. Since it's a function of their job, you are required by law to pay them while they gear up.

Same goes for set up and clean up. If you own a body shop and your employees need to set up for a paint job, they must be on the clock and therefore compensated for it.

On the flip side, when employees take a lunch, they should clock out, eat in your break area, and clock back in as they go to their desk. This sets a nice boundary between work time and personal time. It also prevents you or another supervisor from inadvertently giving an employee work during their break.

This is illegal and should be drilled into your mind, as well as the minds of your supervisors.

You are placing your company at great risk of steep fines, back pay, and lawsuits should you ask an hourly employee to perform work while they are "off the clock." Be sure you train your supervisors and managers thoroughly on this subject!

Withholding Paychecks... A Big No-No!

Whether an employee quits or is fired, it is required by law that they receive their final paycheck. You can't withhold a paycheck; no matter how mad you are at them. This action is sure to bury you in fines, and maybe even land you in jail.

Now, different states have different laws on when a final paycheck has to be given to the employee. Some states require a final paycheck to be given within 72 hours. Some states, including Pennsylvania, require a final paycheck to be given on the next payroll cycle after the termination date (if the employee quits). Some states have different requirements that are based on whether the employee quits or is fired.

It's important that you know your state's laws, so you can play the game inside their constructs.

But no state allows you to withhold earnings without advance permission of the employee. You can find the state by state guide at www.LisaMillerHR.com/vip.

Lisa Kennis-Miller

Section 5
Recordkeeping

Did you know that most employer lawsuits are won on the count of an owner or manager keeping impeccable records?

I realize paperwork isn't glamorous. I understand how its lack of profit-producing ability keeps it low on the priority list. I get it. But. When you have employees, you have to keep good records!

That's why this section will focus on how to do just that: keep good records so that you protect yourself and your business from a future lawsuit and unwanted fines and penalties.

Lisa Kennis-Miller

Document, Document, Document

If you learn nothing else from this book, please follow this piece of advice: Document, Document, Document! Anything that you tell an employee, advise them on, discipline them on, etc., you need to keep detailed notes on.

This CYA maneuver is extremely important because the company is not the only entity that can be sued. You, personally, can be held liable and charged separately as a manager and supervisor in lawsuits.

By documenting everything, if you are in a lawsuit, you can pull out your documentation and show them exactly what happened. In most court cases, it is the documentation that wins the case!

So, how should you document? You can document in a notebook, in a spreadsheet, inside an app (like Evernote), in an email to yourself, or on a voice recorder. It doesn't matter which way you document, as long as you document! Ideally, though, if it is related to an employee, it should be kept in a 'confidential file' under lock and key in HR (or where the rest of your personnel files are kept) but associated with that employee.

Also, be as specific as possible when you're documenting. Write down dates, times, people involved, things said or done, etc. and have witnesses sign the documentation when you can.

However, I encourage you to only write down the facts! It's important to be objective and filter out any emotional ties to an issue, positive or negative.

Think of documenting like a court transcriptionist writes down the notes from court. They don't write down feelings or emotions. They transcribe facts. Who, what, where, when.

By the way, documentation doesn't have to be conflict-oriented. It can also be positive and praise-oriented.

Ok, let me give you two examples of how to write a fact.

Praise-oriented fact: "January 15, 2016: Megan Brown shows up early every morning at 10 minutes till 9:00 AM. Has done this daily for the past 3 months."

Conflict-oriented fact: "On September 18, 2016 at 12:52 p.m., Nate Jones sent an email to his son about their plans for the weekend and spent approximately half an hour of his workday communicating back and forth - which violates company policy. This is the first offense. I warned him about this. We had a discussion. He agreed not to do this anymore."

Notice there are no emotions in either example; just facts about the event or about an observation.

Getting Ahead Of The Game

If you're a go-getter, you could document observations of your employees all year round and get ahead of the performance review game. Think about it. If you documented all year on each employee, your performance review would write itself. You'd have everything you need to sit down and complete your review in a matter of minutes – not hours.

Plus, when you do a performance review once a year without notes, it's unfair to the employee. Listen, you may only remember the most recent things that happened. If they've behaved or have done outstanding recently, then they'll get a positive review. If they've misbehaved – whether major or minor – or done poorly recently, then they may be up the creek without a paddle.

It's not your fault. It's human nature. But you can cut down on this and give them a fair review by documenting your observations all year. For a sample "Critical Incident Log" go to www.LisaMillerHR.com/vip

Lisa Kennis-Miller

The 4-Drawer Method To Keeping Personnel Records Safe

Personnel files must be maintained for each employee and each applicant. In addition, personnel documentation should be kept (and maintained) in four separate files under lock and key at the employer's job site.

The four files are for:

1. Personal Records
2. Medical Records (Confidential)
3. Payroll Records
4. I-9 Forms

Preferably, each file is maintained separately in separate drawers. For example, each employee should have a personnel file in drawer #1, a medical file and confidential records in drawer #2, payroll files in drawer #3, and I-9 Forms in drawer #4.

NOTE: From my experience, the easiest way to maintain I-9 Forms is in a 3-ring binder.

All of these drawers should be under lock and key because they contain birth dates, social security numbers, and private, confidential information.

Lisa Kennis-Miller

As an employer, you are responsible for the protection of the documents and any of the information that you have on our employees; so protect yourself, your employees, and your business by locking up these drawers each and every time you or an employee accesses them.

How Long Should You Keep Records?

Every record has a different length of time that it must be kept on file. Since you need to know this information on a regular basis, I've created a list for you called "How Long Should I Keep That?" You can download it here: www.LisaMillerHR.com/vip

In addition, it's important that you set up and follow a record-shredding schedule. I recommend contacting a shredding company to come into your office and shred documents every year.

Keeping documents after the date they should be shredded is just as dangerous as not having them! Why? Keeping evidence that may incriminate you in any way past the date in which you are required to is just stupid! Plus, if you are not compliant in how you are keeping the records and you decide to store them indefinitely would be a bad idea should you ever be audited by a government agency.

Lisa Kennis-Miller

Time Sheets Must Be What?!

We discussed time sheets in the previous section, but you should also know that all time sheets must be signed by the employee and you (a manager).

The employee's signature is there to verify that their working hours are correct. The supervisor's signature is there to show that they made the effort to determine the employee's hours worked were correct.

Remember, document everything to keep you and your company safe!

Lisa Kennis-Miller

Section 6
Termination

Ok, you now have the tools and resources to hire a new employee, mitigate your risks, properly handle disciplinary actions, hold onto top talent, and keep impeccable records.

In this last section, we'll look at the most dreaded of all responsibilities: terminating an employee.

Terminating an employee is never easy, and it turns most people's stomachs, but it's a necessary evil when you own a business with employees.

We'll also look at why terminating an employee may be the best thing you can do for the future of your business and how to make this process less painful for you and respectful for your soon-to-be ex-employee.

The Band-Aid Approach To Terminating Employees

Terminating an employee is one of the hardest things you'll ever do. I know this from experience. I get a knot in my stomach and can't sleep the night before.

However, it's important that you realize that failure to terminate poor performers or problem employees can have a devastating impact on morale and your company's bottom line!

So, when the time comes to terminate an employee, don't dilly-dally around. Like taking off a band aid, rip it off and get it over with quickly. It's less painful and more productive.

Listen, you may not like it but it's imperative that you do it. You may even feel guilty about it, but don't. After all, employees usually fire themselves (so to speak).

If you have to fire someone, then they did multiple things wrong (maybe even over a long period of time). It's your duty, your responsibility, to save the rest of the employees and your company from their actions.

Lisa Kennis-Miller

Proper Documentation Can Cover Your A$$

As I've said numerous times throughout this book, document everything! When it comes to terminating an employee, make sure you properly document the reason(s) for termination and that it is consistent with your company's policies. In other words, have all your T's crossed and I's dotted before making the decision to terminate someone (unless it is an extreme act which necessitates immediate termination).

We have all seen a movie or TV show where an employee does something stupid and the boss storms in – with a maddening look, face turning purple, steam coming out of their ears – and screams, "You're fired!"

And while that may feel good at the time, we want to avoid something like that at all costs.

Again, it's best to keep your emotions out of this process. Instead, make sure you have a cool head, their behavior and actions properly documented, and your company policies referenced.

Gudger Vs. Citgo

Jackie Gudger was an administrative assistant at Citgo. At a meeting, she got into an argument with a coworker, Health Services Manager Shelby Davis, over a hotel where they chose to host an event. Gudger supposedly said the hotel "sucked" then responded rudely to some questions and derailed the meeting.

In response, Davis asked if Gudger "was ok." Davis later filed a complaint against Gudger for harassment. Gudger responded by filing a complaint against Davis, saying she felt "called out."

When HR investigated, they found that Gudger was the one acting unprofessionally and inappropriately in the meeting, according to others in attendance, and counseled her.

Several other managers had concerns about Gudger's unwillingness to do work assigned to her and in April and May of 2011, she questioned tasks assigned to her. Several coworkers, supervisors, and others said they noticed Gudger's increasingly belligerent attitude between April and October of that year. HR disciplined her for several other incidents and issued a warning for her to improve her attitude.

Gudger then allegedly followed a temporary worker into the parking garage yelling at her on three separate occasions. Gudger was fired shortly thereafter.

She sued, alleging race discrimination, but Citgo moved for summary judgement and showed the court all the disciplinary records. The court determined that Citgo had legitimate, business related reasons for discharging her. It was evident by the extensive disciplinary records and they dismissed the case.

Citgo did everything right. They investigated when they should have, documented each event and terminated the employee when she didn't change her behavior.

Without documentation, this case may have gone further.

("GUDGER v. CITGO PETROLEUM CORPORATION." *GUDGER v. CITGO PETROLEUM CORPORATION*. 3 July 2014. Web. 01 Aug. 2015. http://www.leagle.com/decision/In FCO 20140707089/GUDGER v. CITGO PETROLEUM CORPORATION.)

Lisa Kennis-Miller

When To Terminate Immediately

When the situation warrants, terminate immediately. So you are probably thinking, wait a minute, I thought you just told us to have all our documentation and facts before we act. Now I'm confused.

Let me explain. Say an employee verbally threatened to kill another employee. It would be your responsibility to do a very quick and thorough investigation into the matter and take action before something serious happens. So you investigate, and by that I mean you talk to employees that maybe heard or saw what happened immediately; and maybe several witnesses heard the threat and took it seriously.

You terminate the employee that made the threat immediately, you contact authorities to make them aware of the potential for violence at your workplace, and then you send out a communication to your employees to be on alert for that individual on company property, and if they see him to dial 9-1-1.

You will have done all that can be reasonably expected to protect your employees. You could be in just as much or more trouble for not getting rid of a liability quickly as you would be in for making a hasty decision and firing one that doesn't warrant firing. In a situation like that, if you say, "Okay, we're gonna write you up and warn you this time," and you try to follow progressive discipline, this person could walk in with a gun the next day and kill someone; then you'd really be in trouble!

Can you see why it is very important that when the situation warrants, you can skip all of the progressive discipline steps and fire the employee immediately?

Throughout this book, we've been talking about being calm, careful, and cautious. This "exception" to the rule is no different. You still want to be careful and cautious, but in certain circumstances you must act swiftly.

So, when do you act quickly and terminate someone immediately? When there has been an act of violence committed or when there has been a threat of violence. It could be anything that would potentially threaten your employees, anything that would be an actual or perceived threat of violence in the workplace. It doesn't even have to be some threat to kill. It could be a threat to punch someone, anything that would be racially charged or hate crime-related, any potential threat of violence, that's when you cross into negligent hiring territory that could later be brought against the company in a negligent hiring suit.

Remember, it's your job to protect your employees. Violence or the threat of violence must be taken seriously. Zero tolerance – there should be a policy in your handbook explaining this, too.

Barker Vs. The Boeing Company

Zachary, a male Caucasian, thought it was a good idea to bring a Ku Klux Klan style white sheet, a pointed white hat, a noose, and a stuffed toy monkey into the office one day and confront an African American coworker. The African American coworker immediately reported the incident.

The employer quickly investigated, removed the noose and other items, and fired Zachary.

Zachary sued, alleging the African American coworker had called white coworkers names, like "cracker." Zachary said he suffered reverse discrimination and the investigation should have been more thorough.

The court crossed out Zachary's claim, noting that dressing like a KKK member was far worse than anything that he alleged the African American coworker had done.

The investigation, though not perfect, was good enough.

(Circuit Judge, Brooks Smith. "BARKER v. BOEING COMPANY." Leagle, 14 July 2015. Web. 01 Aug. 2015. http://www.leagle.com/decision/In FCO 20150714085/BARKER v. BOEING COMPANY.)

Lisa Kennis-Miller

Your Quick-Response Team

It's smart to have a "Quick-Response Team" in place for when HR emergencies occur. That way, you can conduct a quick investigation as needed and settle any unique situation before it escalates and gets out of control.

In addition, you may want to make this team responsible for routine reviews of the workplace and making sure racially charged graffiti or props are removed promptly from the office – as well as offensive images or material. Some people are sensitive to what offends them, while others are not. As an employer, it's your job to make sure your employees feel safe in their work environment.

Your Employees Shouldn't Be Confused When Getting Fired

Communication is key. When sitting down with an employee for the "termination talk," you must be clear and you must give them valid business reasons as to the grounds for termination.

Don't talk too much. Get straight to the point. Why are they in there? Why are they being terminated?

Don't argue with them.

Don't apologize.

Don't soften the blow.

Don't call it what it's not.

Don't say they are being "laid off" if they're not.

Don't say their position is being eliminated if it's not.

Tell them they are being fired and the specific reason(s) why they are being fired. Also, don't send mixed signals. Don't praise them for the good work that they did in the past and then fire them. That is conflicting information and can come back to bite you down the road if they initiate a lawsuit.

The best approach is to be straightforward with them. Simply tell them exactly why the termination is happening and lay the documentation out in front of them. Show them the counseling you've tried and the warnings they received.

That should keep arguing to a minimum. They can see what they did and what you did to try to help them and warn them. If they have been warned several times, then seeing documentation in front of them usually makes it click. They can see that they have been given chances to improve.

Last, there's no need to be rude. Be a human being and give them the dignity and respect they deserve. This is the right thing to do…and the safest way to present their termination.

Again, they have to walk out of your office with a crystal clear understanding of what just happened in there. They know what they did wrong and they know that they've been let go.

"Can I Get A Witness?"

It's smart to have another person in the room with you when you terminate an employee. Ideally, this can be their immediate supervisor or another manager.

If you're a small business and don't have any managers or supervisors (other than you), then I highly suggest bringing in an HR Consultant during the termination.

I do NOT recommend having a peer of the person who is being fired in the room – this is awkward. This is a private and confidential meeting.

The role of that witness is to take detailed notes of what is being said and done in the meeting. That way, if there is ever a lawsuit filed, you are protected. The court will know what was said, and by whom. It'll be on record – in black and white.

In addition, be certain that your witness understands exactly what their role is before the employee enters the room.

If the employee asks, "What are they doing in here?" You can simply reply with, "They are here today to take notes on our meeting and act as a witness for the documents."

Last, your disciplinary action forms and your termination forms should have a line for a witness to sign. And, it's smart to have at least one person of the same sex as the employee in the room.

Meaning, if the employee is female and the manager is male, you need to find an appropriate witness that is also female. That way, if the terminated employee ever tries to say that "something happened in the room," you have a witness of the same sex to attest that everything was above-board.

He Who Does The Hiring, Does The Firing

A "best practice" for employers is to have the person who did the hiring also do the firing. This protects your company from the perception of being biased.

For example, if a manager hires an African American employee and 10 months later has to fire that same employee, it is awfully hard to prove bias and wrongful termination if the supervisor that hired him in the first place also is the one who fires him.

If your company is large enough to have a Human Resources department, most of the time the hiring manager is integral in making the hiring decision. Even if your company isn't that big, whoever does the hiring should also be doing the disciplinary actions, the performance reviews, and needs to be involved in any terminations, as well. So it is very important that that manager follow the employee the whole way through their life cycle with the company.

Lisa Kennis-Miller

Another Checklist To The Rescue

Create a termination checklist so nothing is overlooked. The day you terminate an employee is a day of high emotion and chaos. You can't afford for anything to be forgotten.

Termination really does take a great deal of planning and coordination to pull off effectively. If you don't plan it out, then things can and will go wrong.

For example, you go in to work knowing that you have to fire this employee today, but you don't know what time for sure because communication with the manager is poor. Sure as shootin', somebody found out and word starts to spread like wildfire. So now you have to act quickly before it gets back to the affected employee. Things like this happen and because you are flustered, you forget to cut the terminated employee's computer security *(which should be done as soon as they stand up from their desk to come into your office)* and when they come back to their work space to pack things up, they begin a chain of disturbing emails to customers, sabotage files, steal sensitive information, etc.

So if you allow the terminated employee to go back to their work space to pack things up unsupervised, they could (and might) do some real damage. When that ball starts rolling, all kinds of bad things can happen. That's why you really need to have it planned; at least have a checklist of "things you need to do" along the way. Whoever is going to be involved, needs to be in on it. This should be no more than maybe two or three people if you are in a really big company; if you are in a small company it is probably more like one person – and NO ONE else! *This is one of those highly confidential situations.*

You need to think about who's going to be involved, how it's going to be communicated to the remaining staff once the terminated employee is gone, who's going to pick up that person's duties, who's going to answer the calls and emails, etc.

In addition, the final disciplinary action form needs to be written up ahead of time, stating the reason for termination. Keys, ID badges, computers, phones, written documents from the company, etc. must be handed in, as well as a whole list of other important tasks – including COBRA notices if they have health insurance through the company, a termination letter, and final paycheck.

Last, the terminated employee should be escorted by management to gather their belongings and out to their vehicle. Until they are off the premises, they shouldn't be out of management's sight.

Forget any of these things and you could find yourself in trouble – now or down the road. A termination checklist will help you keep things in order, as well as keep you cool, calm, and collected.

Keep Quiet

Terminating someone is highly confidential and saying the wrong thing to the wrong person could prove to be very expensive. Some managers speak too freely about why an employee isn't with the company anymore. There should be no calling of names. You don't want to bring any of your emotions or opinions into that. If someone asks, "What happened to Bob?" – it's smart for you and your managers (who should be trained on what is appropriate to say and what is not) to keep things generic. It will suffice to simply say, "Morgan will not be working with us any longer."

Divulging anything more than a very generic statement could cause a "defamation of character" lawsuit in your future. You don't need to give the exact reason of why someone was fired. It's none of your employees' business. It's your business…and you need to protect your business.

Listen, they are probably going to call Morgan anyway and Morgan is going to give his side of the story. That's fine. Let Morgan say whatever Morgan wants to say. The rumor mill will always be pumping out rumors – your job is to not care.

From the employer's standpoint, your standpoint, take the high road and avoid that "defamation of character" lawsuit. Keep it confidential and keep quiet.

Your Next Steps

Congratulations on taking the first step to laying down a strong foundation for a bullet-proof business! You've learned the basics of what a professional business needs in terms of human resource systems and processes. You have also learned some of the things that can go wrong when you aren't in compliance with the law.

Since I know how hard it can be for a business owner to stay on top of all the human resource issues and new laws, I encourage you to connect with me and continue our relationship on my Facebook page: www.facebook.com/HRRescueResources.com. There, you'll find news and recent employment-related developments that may be relevant to your workplace. In addition, some of the information contained in this book may be outdated by the time you read it, because laws are constantly changing. I encourage you to seek professional help before you make any decisions on employment related matters.

If all this is still a little overwhelming and you'd like some help from me, you can reach me at Lisa@LisaMillerHR.com or by calling me at 724-777-2286.

Sincerely,
Lisa Miller, SHRM-SCP, SPHR

P.S. – Don't forget to download the tools and resources I talked about in this book. They're FREE, so take advantage of them while you can at www.LisaMillerHR.com/vip.

Lisa Kennis-Miller

About The Author

Lisa Kennis-Miller, SHRM-SCP, SPHR, is the Founder of HR Rescue Resources, LLC in Moon Township, PA.

Lisa helps business owners identify vulnerabilities within their organizations that could lead to lawsuits, fines, or other inefficient, unproductive, or costly outcomes and works with them to create or improve HR systems and processes to address problems and improve efficiency.

Her knowledge and experience includes a bachelor's degree in Industrial Organizational Psychology from Penn State University and more than 16 years in corporate human resources ranging from Generalist level work to Senior Management roles.

In addition, Lisa earned a Senior Certified Professional certification from The Society for Human Resource Management (SHRM-SCP) and has a Senior Professional in Human Resources Certification (SPHR) through the HR Certification Institute, signifying her mastery in the principles of human resources and dedication to staying current in the profession.

In Lisa's spare time, she enjoys spending time with her family and friends, playing golf, gardening and baking.

www.ingramcontent.com/pod-product-compliance
Lightning Source LLC
Chambersburg PA
CBHW061438180526
45170CB00004B/1469